The Great Outdoor Competition

by Holly Harper
illustrated by Emma Trithart

Once upon a time there was a girl named Cindy. She loved snowboarding, mountain biking and hiking. Cindy loved being active. She had worn out her shoes outdoors!

Cindy's stepsisters were the complete opposite to her. They hated going outdoors. Instead, they stayed at home. They were much more interested in beauty tips and tricks.

One day, they got a flyer in the mail.

"Yuck!" said Cindy's stepsisters. "Who would want to go to that? You would get all sweaty!"

"I want to go!" said Cindy.

Her stepsisters just giggled. “Poor you! You can’t go. Your shoes are falling apart! Besides, you can’t afford a ticket!”

Cindy had to admit they were right.

Cindy noticed there was a free raffle. The Grand Prize included a ticket to the Great Outdoor Competition. Cindy filled in an entry. She doubted she would win. She might as well try, though.

Early one morning, Cindy heard the doorbell. It was a package addressed to her. Cindy's hopes soared. She read the note. It said, 'Congratulations, Cindy. You have won the Grand Prize!'

There wasn't just a ticket either. The pack contained brand new leggings and a top. Best of all, there were new shoes! Cindy tried them on. They fit her perfectly.

"They're beautiful!" Cindy whispered.

It was the morning of the Great Outdoor Competition. Cindy jumped quickly out of bed. She threw open her wardrobe. Cindy got dressed and ran to catch the bus. She didn't want to be late!

Cindy handed over her ticket. She was so excited. There were all kinds of activities to try. There was mountain biking, rock climbing and skateboarding.

“This is absolutely incredible!” she shouted.

Cindy signed up for a running event. She changed into her new shoes. Then she started to warm up. Cindy hoped the shoes would help her run fast.

"On your mark, get set, go!" called the starter.

Cindy took off running. She felt as though she was soaring down the track. The crowd roared. Cindy came in first place.

Next, Cindy played a game of kickball. After that, she competed in a ropes challenge.

“You’re great at this!” said a boy.

“You were on the flyer!” said Cindy. “Why are you wearing a cap with a crown?”

"I won the competition award last year," said the boy. "I think you might beat me this year, though!"

Cindy did not know who was winning. She was just having fun.

Next up was a tug-of-war. Cindy took off her shoes to get a better grip.

“Heave! Heave!” said her teammates.

Cindy gave it everything she had. The other team toppled forward over the line.

Cindy's phone beeped.

"Oh no! Is that the time? The bus back to town leaves in just a few minutes!" she said.

Cindy quickly packed her bag and took off. She didn't notice when one of her shoes fell out.

A few days later, Cindy was out with her stepsisters. She spotted a long line outside a store.

“What’s going on? Is it a sale?” she asked.

“You haven’t heard?” said her stepsisters.

Cindy shook her head.

"Some girl won the most events at the competition. But she dropped her shoe as she left," said one sister.

"They're looking for the girl it fits. They want to award her the crown cap," said the other.

Cindy's stepsisters joined the line.

"But you weren't even there!" said Cindy.

"So what?" they said. "Maybe we'll get to be on television because we're so beautiful."

The shoe didn't fit Cindy's stepsisters.

The boy grinned when he saw Cindy. "Hey, it's you!" he said. "My name is Tyson by the way."

"Nice to meet you, Tyson. I'm Cindy."

Tyson handed Cindy her missing shoe.

“This belongs to you, too,” he said. He took off the cap and gave it to Cindy. “You won the most events. You are the Great Outdoor Competition Champion!”

"Our sister is famous!" Cindy's stepsisters exclaimed. "That's so cool! Maybe being outdoors isn't so bad after all. Can we come with you to the next Great Outdoor Competition?"

Cindy grinned. "Why wait until next year?" she said. "Let's all go hiking together this weekend! Want to come, Tyson?"

"Absolutely!" said Tyson.

So they all went hiking happily ever after.

Look Back

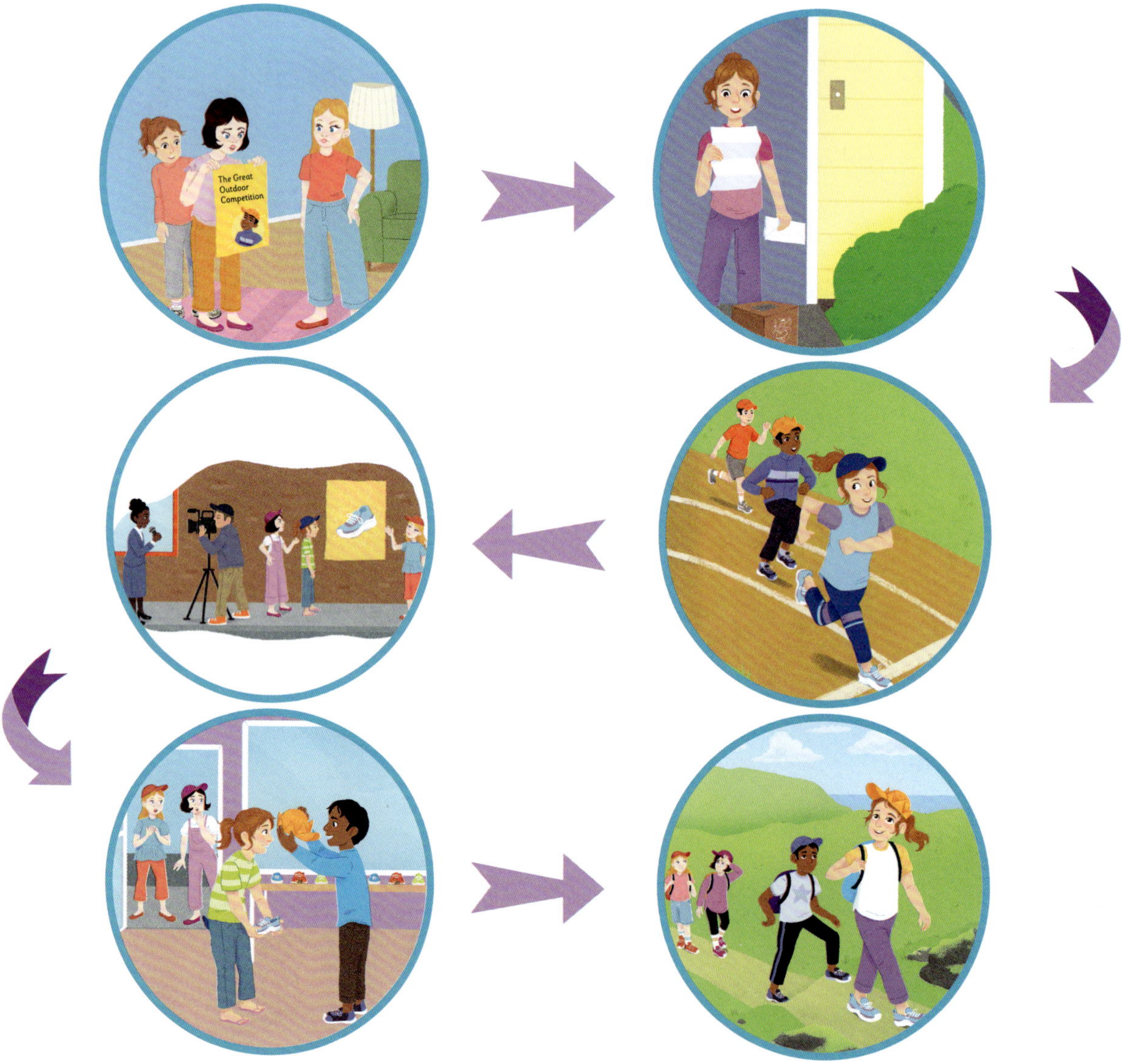

Encourage students to use the pictures to retell the story.